THE LITTLE FIELD OF SELF

PHOENIX **POETS**

A SERIES EDITED BY TOM SLEIGH

THE LITTLE FIELD **OF SELF**

DOREEN GILDROY

THE UNIVERSITY OF CHICAGO PRESS
Chicago and London

DOREEN GILDROY's poems have appeared in magazines such as *American Poetry Review, Ploughshares,* and *TriQuarterly*, among others. This is her first book.

The University of Chicago Press, Chicago 60637
The University of Chicago Press, Ltd., London
© 2002 by The University of Chicago
All rights reserved. Published 2002
Printed in the United States of America

11 10 09 08 07 06 05 04 03 02   1 2 3 4 5

ISBN: 0-226-29328-9 (cloth)
ISBN: 0-226-29329-7 (paper)

Library of Congress Cataloging-in-Publication Data

Gildroy, Doreen.
     The little field of self / Doreen Gildroy.
        p.   cm.—(Phoenix poets)
     ISBN 0-226-29328-9 (alk. paper)—ISBN 0-226-29329-7 (pbk. : alk. paper)
     I. Title. II. Series.

  PS3607.I43 L58   2001
  811'.6—dc21

                                                              2001027563

for my husband

Contents

Acknowledgments

Grateful acknowledgment is made to the following publication in which these poems first appeared:

American Poetry Review: "Afterword," "Dung Beetle," "If All I Do Today Is Change," "If I Could Ask You," "Light Against the Wall," "The Little Field of Self," "Lying on the Bed with the Window Open," "Oh Let Me Be Quiet and Near," "A Rewriting of the Shore," "Stereoscope," "Theology," and "You Take Me to Where."

THE LITTLE FIELD OF SELF

Dung Beetle

Be kind to me, a mess. I represent
persistence—in the
dirty thing;
things larger than me
I do not fear.

Whatever you think, or like—
I live. Oh,
marvel!

Pushing up the hill—
rolling around.
I feel myself at work.

You are larger than I think,
and that is very comforting to me.

The Little Field of Self

Walking up the hill—
What will it be like? I thought.

In another world, in the
golden grass.

Walking up the hill—
with you,
my constant.

Is it seasons, or is it continual
until I say
I know (in part)?

—

How one approaches.
(What action
do I put in it?)

"It's a cloud, will be
in a cloud…"
the monk
warned (anonymously)
but with his
whole being.

—

I didn't see you as far off.
Not knowing language or
landscape.
I couldn't say it was dark.

In My Own Language

A perfect amount of fruit.
Obedient, I begin.

The professor said,
Don't do it the way
I tell you to do it:
Do it right.

—

How I waited!
The impulse, reined.
The letter *was* the morning. Bringing
image and
vacuum.
Mostly giving in
to thoughts and more
thoughts.
A woman writing a letter, and
ripping it up.

—

Someone's momentary
cruelty.
A friend seeking

what does not make him happy.
A chilling lover, recalled.

In the ransacked parts,
in all the warring bodies—

that part of pillar
left standing,
the hand resting quietly
on the waist.

—

An architectural
drawing of a table
(how to build).

Three vases
(what to put in them, what
to admire).

An arch of figures—for over
the door.

—

You tell me, people would think it—
a trip of a lifetime.

It's really *a fine edge
of sanity*, you say,
a castle in the middle of

nowhere,
locked away.

Discovered a place—
everything served over
vine shoots.

The philosopher—in the etching—
(thinking hard) hangs next to
terra cotta lines
of some artist's
God and Man.

———

We came to recollect
a known sleeping and eating.

I didn't come for answer, but dialogue.
I didn't come for even that, except (it is)
my nature. Then

freedom during day
to stop at all those fields to look.

A Rewriting of the Shore

When we walk down
Brittany's savage coast you see
an old stone house you call
dream house—then remember
how cold it would be.

Then your outburst:
You are so wonderful!
I look down and notice
a green sea plant—
unnameable, but mine.

—

Midnight and the ducks
walking along the hedge
of the moat—
squawking away
at some awakening.
Robust in all they say.

Perhaps, before, I had been dull—
preoccupied—separate in my private pains—
and now speaking—
I know it:
fierce.

I am aware, so often,
glancing at your face.

—

Not to be ashamed—
why not take this?

…with you out walking
around the lake and
into the forest where
the geese flee from you
and return.

The birds, clear
in their little way—
yet not pretending everything, and can
anything?
How I love the
odd ends of knowledge.
Better to go lightly along.

If All I Do Today Is Change

> ". . . *as though in a rapture or enthusiasm, he was wholly quiescent . . . in a condition of unmoved calm, with no inclination outward from his own essence.*"
>
> Plotinus—Ennead VI

Sitting, up here, in the loft
hours passing through me—
doing nothing in
particular.

In the garden the cut stalks
feel the wind and
have no resistence to it, moving
and being moved again.

—

If it is
entirely new,
how would I
recognize it?

I wish not to
think of myself
or mere trees!

I don't want to take
the picture or
record.
A friend says:
you give it warmth.
For whom am I
lavishing the landscape?

—

Who of this castle would be king
or thief?
Walking the moat,
the concierge tells of things cast off
and down, the
crown's plucked jewels
and the winged doe
royal symbol.

Within the case
a frayed wire
reconstructs that life
once held in a hand,
bejeweled.

—

So little required of us, today.
Like the fallow land,

like the animals outside
eating and sleeping whatever
the weather.

The palest luminesce
where the gardener had cut severely.

—

Darkest smell of earth.

Trees cracked off
and fallen; the ivy globes
wrapping themselves.

Still cold—
we walk out determined
for the fresh air,

our faces
exposed.

—

For my friend
all day long
I've tried to say it.

Passion has its own history.

Papyrus and parchment,
and the skillful clay.
I examined the maquettes:

spirit-houses, someone's first
House of Soul

before some grand entrance
beyond and beyond.

Must I have
all the volumes
before reading the one!
Perhaps never
ambitious for the next...As if
I never had to
think about it.

Two Figures

I

What were we then and how
shall I think of us
in the future?
I got it in my mind
to take a walk.

In the *couloir*—
the cave key heavy
in my hand—
the cool dampness
of somebody else's life
in the grey stone.
This is where you live now, it says.
I say, *I live in the field.*

II

It's the beginning of something.
Night and day. What does it matter—the grey?

Even day, flat day.
Fed the birds—in sun—finally
warm air and the body free to
flail about.

I have to wear myself out, first.
Such a dark day, then such a lovely one.

You Take Me to Where

everything is growing
out of the wall.

Entering the forest
the light hits the trees—
slanting from the hour.
The moss vibrates in
sun.

You didn't find it
until today, until it was
warm enough to
walk in it.

On the floor of
pine needles, leaves, and sticks
you say, *Take a picture.*
I take:
a fern's
small curling and
uncoiling.

You run around with camera—
taking pictures—in delight—
I'd never seen before.

So many passageways of trees
following the long wall
where everything has decided
to live. (It will live.)

—

This is this story, this time now.
(Because it is a flesh I know.)
The soul, pushed about, finally
stepping out.
Preparing (for a long time)—
writing:
I didn't know what to do. Pain—
I felt the crux.

Waiting on one, living in
the other.
Alternate angles, alternate leaves.
Petrified! What had turned me
to stone? (It was leaving.)
The new took me (I couldn't
have known).
Spiritus asper, spiritus lenis.
Rough breathing, smooth breathing.

Guile

I'll tell you that I like you a lot.

Believe me, it's what I want.
It's what I want.

Oh Let Me Be Quiet and Near

Oh let me be quiet and near.
It's all I can offer.
I've nothing to show—frail,
disrobed.
A world's brokenheartedness.

Whatever else I thought
loses me,
in fever state. Whatever
youth, hard pressed.

I wish to be a silent resting (growing
would be too much to ask)—in my
knowledge. I have none.

Talking as calmly—clearly
as I can. I can't support
it.
You try to tell me your burden—
and I break. Can only weep
today, can only
shake. Not my lack of compassion, rather
all of it.

Acedia

The disappointed self steps forth
(landscape, unchanging)—to
things present, things available.

This Is the Voice of this Life

Hear me, an intuition.
(What you love.)

No longer will I not
tell you about it—all that
most tender desire, secret and
secret again.

Don't take my picture,
not to be exposed (unnecessarily).
Pure—quiet—I'll speak to you.
You don't have to capture
anything. I'll give it, coaxing:
Why don't you show me your face?

Diapause

I don't know where I fall
in this blizzard.
All that time to travel here—
a calm, enforced.
Not disappointment, but shock.

Into the garden
the sepia plants deaden
to themselves.
How will they shed their dense crowns
and the green get
in again?

Coming out of me—
figures of my life's
ghostly grisaille.
Had I forgotten
its grey side? The rat's
daily persistence?

It is beautiful to be looking through
the glass, now
a clear space.

Wanting kindness—above all—
whatever the body felt.

Light Against the Wall

Here, nothing to distract
the snow's embrace.
My life, unchaotic.
The beloved, sought and found.

I will look at my life.

—

These are such quiet hours.
I stare
at the chandelier.
Three lights left, the others
burnt out.

I see them so clearly—still—
when I close my eyes—
all those images burnt into me.

—

Suddenness falling into place—
into the ground,
rising—the whole space—
time (and all that comes
with it).

Why wouldn't I hold
to me
what seemed
most alive? And
take it. Take it swiftly.

—

The heart—the repositing of it—
moving—like breathing
after long illness. (Damp things
let out.)

It's proven
to have taken place while I,
restless, irritable, clung.
Lichen against the wall.

Silva

The animal doesn't
know what I am
and flinches.

———

I didn't know
the names
(what people
called them)
but that
did not persuade me
away
from study.

———

When I wanted to study myself,
I went out the same hour of the day.

When I wanted to study you,
I changed it.

—

Four corners of trees.
Are they the same trees—same
varieties?

Down this road at dusk
I stop to look at the yet
unexplored
at this crossing.

Around me the trees
manifest
in certain light, in
place particular—
this one charcoal; this,
glaucous green—hovering,
honing
my attention.

—

I can't help but reflect.

Only what I stay near
helps me.

Theology

While I was away (the world sorted).

—

Are you going to begin it today? Are you
ready?

Walking to school, singing—a
simple girl, in the field.
The problem sets a form.

—

Subject—always to
limitations.
Stars and heavens
burn their way.
The news tonight: too large.
Am I so vain?
I have always tortured myself
with larger questions—
what to do with death, all
barrenness.

—

Maybe it's different
than I thought:
not a small soul, locked
cell—horsehair
rising on chest,
claiming.

Maybe the animal will come,
whisper.

—

Nothing new under the sun,
but lots of things under the sun.

—

You ask me
to speak more, tell you
of my life. Strange—yet,
you felt curious.

Some parts locked away, some roaming—
or some just quietly
being themselves—not
knowing not to.

You say, *use everything*
(possibly poetry?),
but you mean
the castle, this time—what we
make of it.

Here, in the quiet
of the morning.

—

Enterprise
through the history.
Böhme said, *I am myself
my own book.*
Oh Hound of Heaven.
So many pieces of paper!

—

The very fire—catches
us up. Furiously forging.
Drive to make over
(The already something else).

The book says
kinds of souls, ways
of speaking. How
am I made?
An original soul
rises up, offering its lessons.

—

The wind and leaves,
ever replenishing me.

Different ways,
the book says: *But such as it is,
I have described it as
carefully as I now
am able to do.*

At first I thought it
long and complicated—
but now equally I
could imagine
the child says:
*You think
I'm small, but
I speak to God.*

Eating Apricots

Playful, lighthearted—
a privileged fruit.
An entire bowl!

I gave you a break. Did not
go through my usual
litany. (It's not arrogant,
he knows when
to find me.)

Coda

Yet, little core—you live.
You were aware,
(even then):
how you got here.

New World

"'Come, let it be done', and as I said it, I was on the point of the resolve. I all but did it, yet I did not do it. And I made another effort, and almost succeeded, yet I did not reach it, and did not grasp it, hesitating..."
—St. Augustine

On the first day. The body hardly
can believe it. (That it has
gotten this far.)

This is what has been
given me today.

—

I'm leaving this place—
and where am I going?

Everyday
I live a little more.

Flying over the water
(divined)
I've been there before
(and now I see it).

The navigating
quiet
in my ear.

—

Love, and rooted in it
(whatever variety I am).

The sea grass blooms, discovers
its small fervent bud.

Think of eating fruit. Think of
relieving the guilt—of habit,
of whatever destruction. Within,
without.
It's everything about me.
Watering the bush,
not burning.

—

Sounds calling—
evoking the deer.
I like the stillness at night,
fiery dispensation.

Living in the castle,
I just might start again.

I like being (a little fierce).

—

I had not been praying, had not been
having the best of thoughts. . . .

in the leaves'
corruscated light: a creature
so purely itself (stared with
such purpose).

The time was very long.

What was it—myself?

Lying on the Bed
with the Window Open

Trying to force myself
into somebody else's idea—
what makes a life glorious, or
is the soul bigger than
body—and what did they
think on their beds?

I don't care any longer,
decide to be amused.

I needed to feel myself
as I am, head
upon pillow—to lie down
next to you, image
to rest upon.

I didn't ruin your day.

How the dark thoughts lifted.
Glancing into the book—
for no reason, really.

So that's why I got to see you happy,
dancing around the kitchen singing
"April in Paris"
(on April's first day) concocting "chicken
Michael mango *creme de mure*."

Odd Pieces

I

This downward pulling,
lost and lost
again.

I don't seem
strong enough.

Lash of tongue—withered.

II

I like the wandering days,
in travel.

The accidental find in Carnac
of Menhir and Dolmen.

No one else,
the stones ours to touch—
endearments, faults.

III

Today I feel different, a little.

The rats in the castle, I know
are not the only
life (the life somebody
told you was so).

A workman
pounding at the stones on the
outside wall, doesn't flinch
at the cold.

IV

Because I have
loved well today
I am already beginning
the long comfort I will need
without you
(unimaginable).

Perhaps, cold again
you must tromp around—
scarf twilling around your neck,
holding it all in
(how you feel).

Have all the lessons lost—
this spring—with a
bitter word?

Passion

What's the point of it—if not
peace, if not the arrow's

(entering)
hitting solid center.

If not radiating out—
unquestionable mark, hallowed

precise, perceived
(world opens up):

pierces itself to rest.

Rain

A restless night. Now,
lying in bed with the
murmur of rain
after a day not too
complicated.
(We had decided
not to go out.)

Just stay in, it says,
swirling about,
the noise of it tapping
outside us.
Comfort of another
body. This the design—
and all its powers.

What is it about rain?

As if being taught
mechanical thing,
so intent on directions
(one after another),
we lose all
self-consciousness.

I'll sit at my desk.
Begin to
clear out things.
No task too troublesome.
A willingness
(to give in)
to any conversation.

What Was It?

The scare taunts me
(not to be trusted...).
But the book says:
if sad, it must not scream
or shout.

In the desert, years ago
(almost having lost you):
a day of suffering.
Almost accidentally
you let out a brilliant smile.
The sky, very blue.
Small cloud. Brisk.

I had it in me, before
it happened.

Walking up the stairs—something
coming over me, amused,
no doubt. As in the photos
you are pleased;
radiant.

I like you, being in the
garden. Not a turmoil, not afraid
of gentleness (which was always
your real condition)—sitting
by the water's edge.

I open the window, wave.
What was it? Forgiveness?
More than a little
happiness?

A Mild Turning of the Earth

I am afraid to leave.

I think of your saying,
I don't want to forget
what I learned here.

Bird, chirping in my ear—
as I study myself
in this fierce light, final
self-portrait.

The days, long now—
even into
the time of sleep
here on the latitude of Labrador.

We sit at the moat in two chairs facing out.

The ducks leap out of water,
make their way
into the garden—at a
particular tone
of voice.

I would like to make things
and walk away from them.
Provide a place for this to occur.

Abbey

What I thought
the trip
would be?
So strange here: world yet
different world.

—

Plucking poppies
for my ridiculous
black hat.
Perhaps a festive
attraction toward red.

In the living landscape:
smooth stones, quiet air.

—

Medley of forks, knives.
Select wines—and the
unidentifiable
flat spoon.
Oh bark of tree!
pressed to my
silver plate.

An elegance, giving
gifts. What I learned of
two kinds, the
cultivated,
and the raw.

—

With the saw
they cut into rock,
following plan.
The master builder's rule:
cool lines.

In my prayer,
I did nothing. Rested,
moved along.

It wasn't that he wasn't
trying to make something
beautiful (when he sent
the trinkets away):
St. Bernard
dared
tools, stone.

—

His book assures us:
it's not just the ruins, it's
what he
made of it.
Everything smells lavender;

driving through. In the tabac shop
I remember
how a certain
bitterness could be.

———

Just as a particular place
in the forest once
struck me as home,
other things do,
taking a very different turn,
(perhaps more
glorious) released,
like telling the truth.
All new species of grasses
at my feet.
A voice saying,
joys, there—
awaiting you.

Stereoscope

Actually the trip is when
I come home—that the food seems
most voluptuous. Odd-bodied turnips,
their iridescent leaves flowing over
a tray. (Simple still life.)
At the table, I look out
the window at the familiar crane,
sensitive to my every move—
even through distance.
Is it daydream? or merely
animal being as it is.
Oh strange occupation!
It is always
of color—this animal noise—
always a season
and time.
Today the fresh tulips
(I brought in), the plate of pears.

While You Were Away

A friend says,
There's nobody home. Maybe
you're supposed to
spend this time
alone.

Your letters, messages—
I take them everywhere.

Driving out today
in the chaparral's
quiet open, place.

I'm planning
our garden—the idea,
here and now—
small investigation.

Terra cotta pots
contain everything:
the vibrant cuttings, their
redolent roots.

Yet, they must ask:
Show me something different, now—
take me there.

I dream
Mendel and the peas—
tendrils green with
a certain fondness
from childhood;
a devotion, long hid.

It was not a pleasure I
had planned for.

In the fullness of summer,
great longing.

Epigraph

It's not missing, it's gone.
What year is this, and
who am I?

To whose purpose, I do not know.
Just for the glory of it.
(I am not the first.)

The sound of your voice!

I began to act differently.
(It's what I could do.)

Catalogue of Notebooks

I

I remember being very tired, someone
being kind.

Opening the books:
this elegy.

I understand it
as best I can.
Remnants I will never
destroy again.

II

From one gone before,
the dead speak, the
dying.

Forgive my faults, what I couldn't see.
Change me, as you will.

I am not the first to have these feelings.
Maybe there was a reason I hesitated.

III

What my constants are,
an evenness, a power.

No matter what one may be
obsessed by, (caught)
its own trilogy led.

It must be intimate. Clear
in its calling.

IV

On my desk (in our house)
the artist's notes (what
he looked at)
etching in
tiniest of landscapes—
I loved instantaneously (though
knowing nothing).

The soul recognizes
what is real,
wants to go there.

V

They've helped my life
continue on;
with what they did,
they beckoned.
Reflected,
they seem spirits.

Botanical trees and leaves—
cameo
of a child-bird
and urns. Work
that went on
before
I was born.

VI

From the notebooks
to here—displayed
painting of *Two Poets*.
Is it laurel
in the background?

There could be endless
interpretations,
and I'll take mine—
bread and wine,
oyster shells, bag
of red markings.

Sitting together on the bench
(who can understand completely?)
they both hold on,
looking out.

VII

I have come
to learn
how others see things
(myself intact).

Perhaps all those things you say
are true. Perhaps, not displeasing
(as I thought).

What is the age of
the spirit?

I must live
where I thrive.

It's time I lived in
the age
I was born into.

VIII

I think I'll let
the history
say it for me.

(This is where I live now,
with you.)

Maybe you're different
than I think;
and maybe I'm different
than I think.

A little flesh, a little breath.

I wrote this book
out of this life.

If I Could Ask You

If I couldn't recognize
myself
I couldn't recognize you.

Walking up the hill—
on the still wild landscape

the golden mustard seed
reflected the low evening light;
the red weed bent

for the inclusion of our
human presence.

And then I forgot myself,
and the long figuring out

and took delight in you—
and was
myself: delighted.

Afterword

I want to be bold enough
to say it. *I don't know
what will come
after that.*

Soon it will be spring.
You start to live in it.